Dazed
Dazzled
Dead

John Hudson

A Markings Publication

ISBN 978-1-901913-28-6

This edition prepared, designed and typeset
by the author

www.johnhudson.info

A CIP catalogue record for this book is available from
the British Library

Markings,
Quillet,
Castle Douglas,
DG7 3EL
United Kingdom

Markings

Also by John Hudson

Rogue Seed
Notes from Nowhere
The Road Taken
111 Little Love Poems
13 Souls in Search of a Light Switch
Earth
SHED
The Pumpkin Lantern, Selected Poems 1985-2003
Garden of Love
A Rose by Your Heart
Towards the Sea
Star, Wood, Stone
In Town Tonight, anthology
Medusa Muse
A Greek Phrase Book

Other work by John Hudson

Poetry Surprises, YouTube channel
Toutes Directions, film installation (with Chrys Salt)
Au fil d'Ecosse, installation (with Cyril Barrand)
The Voyage of the Philomel, installation
Spirit of Greatness, exhibition
Solway Fire, 6 films on Dumfries and Galloway writers
Across the River, short film
Prononcez Coeur-Cu-Brie, film
Wednesday's Girl, short film

As Editor

Markings Magazine, 1995-2010 (30 issues)
12 Galloway Poets
The Collected Poems of William Nicholson
The Brownie of Blednoch by William Nicholson
Poems of James Clerk Maxwell
Round About Burns

John Hudson is the author of several poetry collections, and a creator of poetry installations as well as films and other artwork based around poetry. Former editor of the literary magazine, *Markings*, which he founded, John has also edited poetry anthologies and collections. He has performed his poetry to acclaim in a lively, informal and colloquial style to audiences around the world. From 2002 to 2015 he was a Director of *The Bakehouse*, a poetry performance space in Scotland. Winner of literary awards, including two SAC writers' bursaries, John has held writing fellowships in France, Ireland and Shetland. He helped establish the town of Wigtown as Scotland's National Book Town, and he has conceived and directed many transnational arts projects between Scotland and France. His YouTube channel, *Poetry Surprises*, presents his own work, the work of other poets and engages with poetry techniques and topics of the day. He also writes articles for journals and websites, specialising in but not limited to the culture of the library worldwide and information science. John divides his time between living and working in Scotland, London and France.

Find out more at: www.johnhudson.info
Visit John Hudson's Poetry Surprises:
www.youtube.com/user/johnhudson111

I'd like to thank those who have given me the time, space and means to work on this book, especially Lesley.

i.m. James Whyte

Clocks struck the hour
And struck this humble man;
We watched a little hand
Effortlessly overpower
Friendship, hope and trust
Into lifeless dust.

For Cameron

CONTENTS

Dead

Epilogue

ANTHEM

All stand for Planet Freedom,
Hurtling through Deep Space,
Guardian of her children
Called the Human Race.

May Providence protect her
From terrible Black Holes,
And Science prove Defender
Of umpteen billion souls.

Sing! Sing, O Mighty Mountains,
Arise and sing aloud,
Proclaiming Planet Freedom,
Fearless, Strong and Proud!

Emboldened by bright Reason,
Intellect is Guide
In lands where brute Emotion
Finds no cave to hide.

Let no man covet Power
Beyond the Power of State
Or let him meet his hour
When falls an awful Fate.

Sing! Sing, O Mighty Oceans,
Arise and sing aloud,
Proclaiming Planet Freedom,
Fearless, Strong and Proud!

May Fortune crush Misfortune
And Order conquer Strife,
With Righteousness the surgeon
To wield sweet Virtue's knife.

We'll excise cruel Injustice
And Vanity's rude show,
Then amputate vile Avarice
To let sweet Justice Grow.

Sing! Sing, O Mighty Ice Caps,
Arise and sing aloud,
Proclaiming Planet Freedom,
Fearless, Strong and Proud!

May Wealth disperse her riches
Around the Free World's girth
And serve up daily dishes
Grown in wholesome Earth.

With Charity our Banner
Dispensing surplus Hope,
We'll airdrop Freedom's manna
To those who cannot cope.

Sing! Sing, O Mighty Angels,
Arise and sing aloud,
Proclaiming Planet Freedom,
Fearless, Strong and Proud!

May Guns defeat the Tyrant
And Bliss extend her reign,
To silence every miscreant
That threatens with Disdain.

With Wrath our awesome canon,
Dignity our shield
And Truth our final weapon
We're sure to take the field.

Sing! Sing, O Mighty Armies,
Arise and sing aloud,
Proclaiming Planet Freedom,
Fearless, Strong and Proud!

May Faith be bred in Purity,
May hearts rejoice in Good;
We will defend our Liberty
Until we're Understood

And Vice sent to Perdition
Where vile Resentment dwells,
As we give loud rendition
And our Anthem swells.

Sing! Sing, O Mighty Nations,
Arise and sing aloud,
Proclaiming Planet Freedom,
Fearless, Strong and Proud!

And when we face Extinction
As Planet Freedom dies,
We'll stand with one Conviction:
God was on our side.

Our End was Evil's doing,
That Dragon of the Night,
Its Hubris kept accruing
Death. But: WE WERE RIGHT!

Sing! Sing, O Mighty Corpses,
Arise and sing aloud,
Proclaiming Planet Freedom,
Fearless, Strong and Proud!

Dazed

SILENT SONG

I saw a bolt of lightning
Although the sky was blue.
I squeezed my hands upon my ears,
No clap came crashing through.

Was that silent lightning
Forking feet from me?
No bang, no fizz, no thunder smash,
Just whiteness by that tree.

I close my eyes to check
And there's the afterglow
Then kneel to touch the cindered earth
Struck a blink ago.

Why did I not hear it?
Perhaps it struck me deaf
But silent lightning changed the way
Songs run through my head.

RIDDLE

Who is deadly
But persuades she's friendly?

He employs disguises,
But mimicry hides surprises.

She may fool writer more than reader
For she loves the self-deceiver.

He's a cartographer crazed,
Renames roads to leave us dazed.

She is significantly rarer
Than critics ever declare her.

Those that know him change to moths
Dazzled by white tablecloths.

She sets the heart to pumping fast
Until it stops. At last.

SAGE SONG

They say deep wisdom comes with age
But is this really true?
How does a fool become a sage
If follies they accrue?

But sages claim it's true
To say deep wisdom comes with age
From follies they accrue.
That's how a fool becomes a sage.

So if a fool becomes a sage
From follies they accrue,
To say deep wisdom comes with age
Is folly if it's true.

If follies they accrue
Become both fool and ageing sage,
Do sages know what's true?
They say deep wisdom comes with age.

MY SONG

You can beat me when I'm down
You can run me out of town
Sure I done you wrong
But don't take away my song

Don't take away my song
That's been there all along
Before I saw your eyes
And fell for fortune's lies

Don't give a damn for me
But singing sets me free
It's more than gold or fame
More cherished than my name

My song is sung for you
Without it we are through
I sing to make us strong
Don't take away my song

Don't take away my song
That's been there all along
Since first our sunlight shone
And words flew off a tongue

Best pack my bags and go
You won't enjoy the show
When madness comes along
Because you stole my song

THE WANDERER

It's a melancholy night
And I'm feeling deadly down
Once my world was full of light
Now it's all a shade of brown

Gotta take my backpack
And get on out of town
Leave my lady sleeping
'Neath a quilt of eiderdown

Yes, I'm running from her
To a land that's grim and grey
As rain runs down my cheekbone
Into six dark feet of clay

I have to keep on moving
From sun into the storm
And watch the fateful lightning
Strike another dawn

In a land where no-one knows
About the lives I've led
And I can keep on dreaming
In sleep among the dead

I'll lie upon a tombstone
And sing about my strife
Telling ghosts that listen
I've lived a stranger's life

Wandering a bleak land
Always on the run
Afraid of human kindness
And of love to come

Each faltering step is hopeless
Has been since my birth
So I lock my heart away
And trek a joyless earth

MURDER VERSES

There's a bloke in the kitchen
And he's not here for his lunch
There's a bloke in the kitchen
With a bald pate and a punch

The kitchen door's wide open
His torso's hard and green
I don't know why he came here
But he's ugly and he's mean

Before I go to face him
I've had this dream before
Back then I killed the geezer
Got hunted by the Law

But *this* bloke in the kitchen
Is evil head to shoe
He's gonna kick and punch me
Until I'm red and blue

FAIRY TALE

Step back from the edge,
Return to the trodden path.
Don't spoil your patent leather shoes
And lose that carefree laugh.

What was it drove her onward,
Regard me with disdain?
Didn't she know a toe in the mud
Will suck her like a drain?

I told her stick to the track.
OK, for sure, look back,
But never to where the elves
Of impossible selves

Tempt you for you'll trip
In those shiny lampblack shoes.
Then calf to knee to hip,
Belly, breast then lip

The elves will tug you down
Into the boggy slack
Till your eyes gaze back
As you gutter, gag and drown.

SONG OF FORTUNES

Stell was ace at hockey,
She made the GB team
Then married Pete and got divorced
But Alfie came between.

Straight from work at Tesco,
She picks up Alf from school,
Drives twenty miles for training
At the Olympic swimming pool.

And outside every playground
There's queues of mums and dads
Hoping that their offspring
Find fortune from their fads.

Stell invests the money,
Alf blitzes every test;
Mum parades him proudly
With medals on his chest.

Then Alf wakes up one morning
And won't swim any more;
Stell's in bed with a jealous bloke
And Alfie's out the door.

And lives pass in this manner
In early onset regret:
He could have been a striker
But he's stuck behind the net.

Alf thinks he'll be an artist
But Guidance gives advice:
Bohemian life's uncertain,
Clerical jobs are nice.

His medals in a shoe box,
Alf works in debt relief.
Stell's involved with a married man
Who gives her endless grief.

And lives pass in this manner
In early onset regret:
He could have been a striker
But he's stuck behind the net.

Then Alf meets Sharon Bakewell
And soon they have three kids:
Football, Hockey, Swimming,
Each with first team bids.

Alf moonlights doing bar graft,
Shaz blows his hard-earned cash
Taxying the kids to train
Until she's in a smash.

And outside every playground
There's queues of mums and dads
Hoping that their offspring
Find fortune from their fads.

Alfie proves unfaithful,
Shaz ODs on pills;
The kids become statistics
That measure social ills.

Swimming drowns in ketamine
Hockey covets fame,
Football makes the local squad
Although his footwork's lame.

And lives pass in this manner
In early onset regret:
He could have been a striker
But he's stuck behind the net.

Consumed by guilt and gambling,
Alf boozes nights away
But Saturdays he's in the stand
To watch the *Wanderers* play.

With *Wanderers* relegated,
His boy's kicked from the team
But Hockey's pumping botox
And posts she lives the dream.

And outside every playground
There's queues of mums and dads
Hoping that their offspring
Find fortune from their fads.

Alfie gets demotion,
Hockey's on parole,
Swimming gets a headstone,
And Football's on the dole.

Stell's stuck in a care home
And screams to wake the dead,
A photo of her granddaughter
Cracked beside the bed.

And lives pass in this manner
In early onset regret:
He could have been a striker
But he's stuck behind the net

While outside every playground
There's queues of mums and dads
Hoping that their offspring
Find fortune from their fads.

SONG OF HEALING

Put all that pain behind you
Let the river take its course
Don't let regret remind you
Of the hurting at its source

Once we drank sweet waters
Then drinking them turned sour
There's no return to starters
Our lives are in this hour

Right now your world is frozen
Your breath hangs in the air
Compassion hasn't chosen
To melt that icy stare

Feel the sunshine up there
To warm that ice away
And then the river can repair
The hurt that mustn't stay

Let all that pain behind you
Join the river on its course
And let your heart relieve you
Of the hurting and its source

PAIR OF SHOES

Walking across the car park
Just before it gets dark
Walking across the car park
To buy a pair of shoes

Walking close together
As if it was forever
Walking close together
To buy a pair of shoes

Holding hands like lovers
Newly with each other
Holding hands like lovers
To buy a pair of shoes

Wishing that the car park
Just before it gets dark
Wishing that the car park
Promised more than shoes

Stopping at the glass door
Just outside the shoe store
Stopping at the glass door
To buy a pair of shoes

Kissing under new stars
There are no more parked cars
Kissing under new stars
They forget about the shoes

CROW'S NONSENSE

The moon
Is many moons -
As many as men
That gaze upon it.

The earth is blue,
The earth is dark,
Depending on who's
Above or below it.

Apples fall
On the shadow hill;
Nobody gathers them,
Nobody will.

And men in frock coats
Sail a salty old boat
To lands astronomers
Call remote

That nobody owns
Where nobody reads
But corny love lyrics
Trouble the dead.

Dark crow cried
As the big bomb blew
And the rhymester died
As the ocean dried

And the lover sighed
As the boat ran aground with its crew,
Boo-hoo.

So, what sang the crow,
Don't you know?
Don't you know
The maid leaves nothing to you
Or you
Except the bang of a bomb
And a Chinese gong
With a serving of Danish stew,
A few grains of pollen
Peat and a match,
Some pepper and salt
On dry bread down the hatch
And a compass and crew
For a trip on a skiff you can't catch?

The ghost in the boat
Gave the crow a short note
Which the crow
Recited aloud:

Take these words
Says our capt'in,
To use as you see fit.
Nothing's mine,
Neither this nor that line,
Neither moons, silver spoons
Nor a ring-a-ding chime
Nor a lightning struck rhyme,
Nor the sea, nor a path

Nor a trip on a raft
Nor a tractor slicing the land
Like sand;
Be you lame, be you fit
Only clowns have bright wit
Though their lamps can't be lit
Cos the matches have soaked up the stew,
It's true.
And the fool isn't king,
For a see-saw's the thing
That giddies both monarch and you.
Wake up glad, likely lad,
The maid is not mad
For she lacks a black eye
Gummed with watery glue.

And that, said wise crow,
With a starship in tow,
And a faggot ablaze in the pit
Must be the end, o yes the end,
The very end of it!

SONG OF THE PASSENGER

The willow herb stands out today
Along the rusty railway.

That bloke looks shit
Clambering into his Transit.

Next seat's neat-freak nibbling a banana
Doesn't have a bright mañana.

The sun's peeped out;
Presage, *sans doute*, of drought.

I bet she's one for dinner parties,
Passing petit-fours to arties.

These trees - don't know the name -
Like in my garden, apart but same.

To think that pooch is partly me
As are molecules in the sea.

Things can only get better or worse
In an expanding universe.

We're all loco, lacking motive,
Pulled behind a locomotive.

At last, the platform slides to stop.
One by one, off we hop.

SONG OF THE CITIZEN

In bed watching *Breakfast*,
Just had a rotten dream,
So put the night behind me
With Naga and the team.
Come tomorrow, come what may,
I'm living day to day.

The weather's like a monsoon,
But Carol forecasts drought.
The chemist's out of sunscreen
So dare not venture out.
It's worse than ever, have to say,
I'm living day to day.

Democracy defeats me -
I voted for Remain -
And every damned election
My ballot's cast in vain
And so I'll never have my way,
Frustrated day on day.

I cannot flee to Europe,
England's seen to that;
It proudly got its borders back
With FUCK OFF on the mat.
My feet are stuck in UK clay,
I'm sinking day to day.

The trains won't stutter forward,
Freight piles high in ports,
Potholes pepper motorways
And baggage clogs resorts.
I think it's clear, I'm forced to stay,
Queuing day on day.

My motor needs some spark plugs,
Supplies are running short
So the garage leaves the old ones in
And now the car's kaput.
They towed the smoking wreck away,
I'm walking from today.

Water's being rationed,
Shit flows past my door,
The pipes are leaking profits,
Utilities charge more.
The Chairman's getting bonus pay;
I'm drowning day to day.

My Direct Debit's sky high,
I can't afford the rent
The price of oil has rocketed,
My savings are all spent.
A Catholic would kneel and pray,
Ave Maria, Maria ave.

I eke out my resources
Till mildew's on my bread,
I've cut out eating breakfast
And lunch – in fact, I stay in bed.
Can I draw some cash today?
No blinking way José.

I cannot get a dentist,
The doc's agenda's full
I hope I don't need 999
Cos no-one takes the call.
The only option is to pay
To live and breathe another day.

With bosses short on money,
The workers are on strike;
We're told there's nothing to be done
So best get on your bike.
Every worker wants a raise
And a cut to working days.

Our leaders are all liars,
They calculate and spin
Till we're turning round in circles
Just to save our skin.
If you'll let me have my say,
I'm silenced day on day.

And why have half the people
Adopted clowns as kings,
And set the wolves of hatred loose
As anger pulls their strings?
I can't abide the news, okay?
I play the ostrich day on day.

And now we're fighting Putin
It seems he's lost the plot.
We're selling arms like sweeties
Until we all get shot.
Come on lads, join the fray,
Start dying day on day.

I'm told it's getting hotter,
The poles are melting fast
And forests burn like matchsticks
Till Earth will breathe its last.
I watch the climate in dismay,
Sweating buckets day on day.

Of course, then there's Covid...
You know, I near forgot.
We're confident we've beat it
So probably we've not.
In the end, I have to say
Life's not worth the day to day.

I can't reboot my laptop
Since ransomware took hold
And AI is the end of, well,
Everyone I'm told.
Alexa has the final say
"Why not end it all today?"

So, I rig the meter
And leave a note: *Goodbye!*
Seal the door, switch out the light
Then turn the gas on high.
I had to go, I couldn't stay;
All I had was yesterday.

Dazzled

EPITHALAMION

For Cliona and Cameron

*It would be an empty universe indeed if it were not
for the people I love.*
                    Stephen Hawking

I'm reading Stephen Hawking as I fly
Across the world in shadow six miles high;
Black holes, pulsars, mass and awkward quarks
Swill with canapés and popping corks.

Up here I've room to pause and rationalise
Everything from God to swatting flies;
Such lofty thoughts and booze at altitude
Leave me, briefly, like a man renewed.

Here's reason why inebriation's good:
It helps ignore the trees to see the wood.
And so, I jet across the wine-dark sea
To honour two as one joined happily.

The birth of matter, time, of near and far,
Every blade of grass and burning star
Can be expressed as hand fits glove:
The force that binds it all is known as love.

In love we have no need of explanations,
No need of mathematical equations;
A kiss expresses all we need to know
And with that kiss a star begins to glow.

Atoms join, a cosmos comes to life
And in that cosmos husband marries wife.
So, Cam, my son in all but name and seed,
Cliona, daughter, through this happy creed,

May love that bore the stars be yours as guide
And may your love enlighten all our skies;
Let no black hole obscure your happiness,
No quarks or chilly bosons make you less.

Yours is the earth, the cosmos, yours all time;
Enchanting song beyond my reason's rhyme.
The physicist discovers mundane things
While lovers fly above on timeless wings.

STAR GAZER'S SONG

Watching through my convex eye,
Closer I gaze, swifter you fly.

Hold Venus close, fight with Mars.
There, then gone. Likewise stars.

Nebulae, galaxies? Slippery discs.
Don't be fooled, nothing sits.

Giddy in my garden, lying back,
I focus hard on stationary black.

SONG OF THE NIGHTINGALE

Nightingale singing
Singing in the siding
Sat in an ash tree
Singing to the stars

Singing to the moon
Singing to the woodland
Singing to his sweetheart
Several fields away

Singing by my pillow
Deep in my dream tree
Singing for his soulmate
Listening from afar

Singing from the blackness
Darkness deep around him
Singing like a solar flare
To leap the blinding night

Sing along the towpath
Sing beside the railway
Sat in your dream tree
Sing all night for me

THE PATH'S QUESTION

Listen to the night, as you walk
From home to pathway's fork;
See tracks you never took
And those that you mistook.

Watch for the invisible hand
That guides you as you stand.
Which footpath shall you take
Across the boundless lake?

ADVENTURER'S SONG

Even 'though you're stuck at home
Imagination starts to roam:
Feel the river through your toes
Knowing it's the tap that flows,
Sniff sweet honey in the air
Though no bees are ever here,
Catch the skylark's trilling song
Or donkey's eeyore loud and long
Even as you turn and call
To the mirror in the hall;
Taste the strawberry in the woods
Rambling through your cupboard foods
Or watch as silver raindrops streak
Down the window of your cheek
And dream you lie beneath the sun
Dozing with the light-bulb on
Then follow trails of shooting stars
Cast by beams from passing cars
While, boiling water for some tea,
The kettle's raucous energy
Propels you through the galaxy.

THE FLY AND THE SPIDER

"Do not complain," said Spider,
And the fly complied,
Wrapped up in his silken gown
He froze and meekly sighed.

"Do not sigh," said the spider
And Fly looked back and smiled,
In hope of spider sympathy
But Spider laughed, then cried:

"Do not blink your hundred eyes,
The eight of mine will see
If any fang or hair or flank
Or one of your six stumpy shanks
As much as twists or writhes
In hope of getting free."

"But why do you distrust me so?"
Asked the helpless fly.
"Is it something I have said
That keeps me dangling on a thread?
Is it something that I know?
Or do my pearly wings that glow
Sentence me to die?"

"Now I shall spin strong threads of silk
And tighten them for spite.
No gaoler's ever been so kind
To gift you breeks that royally bind.
Your monstrous lack of gratitude
Is what denies you flight."

So Fly sang praise to Spider
In thanks for such fine clothes
But as his song grew louder,
Spider sniffed his nose.

"Do not sing on," said Spider,
"There's nought to sing about."
But try as hard as Fly might,
Fly notes kept popping out.

"That's it!" said angry Spider,
"I'll suck you till you're dry
And shrunken to a withered husk.
Then peace will comfort me at dusk."

"I cannot stop," sang singing Fly
And Spider spat in rage.
He stamped on the threads of his silken web
With first his fourth then seventh leg,
And the eighth came clattering down
In hammer strikes of arachnid sound.

But no amount of drumming
Could drown out Fly's sweet song.
So Spider plucked his silken strings,
Arpeggioed up to the flightless wings
Smartly dressed in homespun rings,
But when his eight eyes searched around
The breeks that he had tightly wound
Clothed nothing but angelic sound.
Fly was nowhere to be found.

SUCCESS

Someone said, "Don't waste your life."
I'm sure that this was sound advice.
While helping friends I could be
Writing a masterpiece. Seriously?
While I'm drinking too much wine
I could earn a fortune. Fine.
More driven me could be PM,
Running NASA, crème de la crème,
Or Poet Laureate, published at least.
Impressive, I guess. Thanks for the belief.
I've heard it since the balding Head
Leant over me and sternly said:
Hudson, you are Oxbridge stuff.
Sorry guv. Enough's enough!
Something in me struggles to believe
Great success leads to great achieve.
So, I'll help my friends, drink my wine,
Laugh, be thankful, end-stop this line.

RESPONSORIES

Here's the big-time, let it through;
Prize by prize, it's choosing you.
Each new prize that comes to be
Makes an emptiness of me.

Halls of silver, plates of gold
For the taking, if you're bold.
Where's the unaccounted fee?
Taking doesn't make it free.

Invest in art; it's bound to pay.
But not the artist, dare I say?

Do come round for scones and tea.
Sorry, scones are not for me.
Then try some vintage port and cheese.
You'll find my stomach disagrees.

You have to learn to play the game.
Or resign, rejecting fame
Or forget you have a name
Or just die – it's all the same.

Then say a prayer and meet your Maker
Of whom I'll ask no grace or favour.

BOOKSHOP RAP

Went down to my bookshop to buy
The first book cover to catch my eye.
Life's a chance, always at play,
So let life answer a question today.
Here's some bloke I've never heard
Crazy 'bout a leather-clad bird.
I'm pumped up by the rainbow language,
Get dazzled by a lightning image.
His beat's a breakdance, naked and free,
Leaves unwrap on my rapper tree.
I like that shock. I'll have shot,
Rap a bit, loosen up, stop my rot.
Leaf through pages, get a head shake.
Pot-luck covers rap you awake.

ICEBERG BALLAD

Weeks of Arctic cold,
Great Britain blanches;
Fields of ice take hold,
A fissure branches.

Blokes back from work,
Stand like awks and gawp;
They feel the crack and jerk,
The awful birthing gap.

Chingford the calving point,
Wood Street to The Bell
Yawns a chasm out of joint;
We drift and wave farewell.

Our burghers head past Sheppey
On an ice-sheet so slow
They're all feeling sleepy,
And go with the chilly floe.

Ta-ta Dover, *hola* France,
Bonjour Gib, *ciao* Funchal,
Conflicting currents swirl and dance
Around our ferry glacial.

Some sing *hallelujah!*
The UK is no more,
While Tories count their moolah
Upon a foreign shore.

The Sun reports that Glasgow
Is drifting north of Yell,
Wales is now Morocco
And Belfast's back in Hell.

London's piled up wreckage
But Essex still floats proud
Denying any breakage
Beneath its icy shroud.

With Thurrock seat of power
And Southend last resort,
No foreign force can cower
The Fleet in Tilbury port.

Boffins can't discover
Why Dagenham is fixed
While all of Rule Britannia
Drifts up swanny Styx.

And as my icepop reaches
The warm Caribbean,
Bumps into tequila beaches
Where grows the coffee bean,

I thank the berg that shifted
From white, unpleasant lands;
It's melt has gladly gifted
Sunshine, sea and sands.

MONEY'S SONG

Never had much. Always enough.
Money is such funny stuff.
Want some, loads, ever more?
For me it's in and out the door.

Some have moolah without end,
Piles of cash they cannot spend.
But for me, it just pours out
Until my bank announces drought.

No money and your spirits drop.
No money and your life's full-stop.
Best give yourself a gambler's chance
And ignore your bank balance.

Do you really need to know
The ebbing tide of your cashflow?
When in the red think nothing of it.
Die in debt, make a profit.

COMPLAINT

Don't need airs and manners,
Don't need a Parker pen,
And I don't need a set of spanners,
Or a toolbox to put them in.
(Even if I drive a Citroën.)

I don't need expensive handwash,
Don't need Levi jeans,
I don't need Apple AirPods,
Nor tins for Whittard teas.
('Though my partner disagrees.)

I can't be arsed with dining fine,
Don't give a sod for fancy fobs
And under gold, I draw a line,
Prefer to undertake odd jobs.
(Poets give and bankers rob.)

It's no to hoity people
And dogs are off the scale
And seeing all chiels equal
I'd rather be in jail.
(Or a penthouse off the Mall.)

Power's not an option -
Authority? That sucks.
And fame is a concoction
For hyperactive shmucks.
(I'd rather drive a garbage truck.)

Don't want fancy trainers,
Don't want Hendrick's gin,
A Rolex? Come on. No brainer;
Find a bin to put it in.
(Worthless piece of tin.)

No, what I need is peace
And no more grab and shove;
My time is on short lease -
DAMN ORDERS FROM ABOVE!
I would sing of love.

CHAMPAGNE ANARCHIST

When you don't believe in anything
It's easy to agree
With black or white or blue or brown
Or any shade between:
He's a champagne anarchist
As you, my friend, will see.

He'll stand for truth but tell a lie
The truth it ain't for him;
He much prefers the tallest tale
Based on sudden whim,
For he's a champagne anarchist
Who only deals in spin.

He doesn't care for luxury,
Condemning wealth as sin
But fine hotels and caviar
Keep on finding him.
Yes, he's the champagne anarchist
With unselfconscious grin.

Rejecting class and power
He claims we're all born free
But treads upon the next man
Who wants his liberty,
For he's a champagne anarchist
And that's what matters - "me".

He doesn't like religion,
It's rank hypocrisy
But often visits churches
To never bend the knee,
For every champagne anarchist
Inverts his Rho and Chi.

Despising all do-gooders,
He mocks them cruelly
But helps a blind cat cross the road
And gives it cream for tea,
For he's a champagne anarchist
Whose love is given free.

He cannot stand the canon
Of litera-ta-ti
But praises all his favourites
Like Petrarch and Dan-tee,
For such a champagne anarchist
Non-sequiturs *così*.

And never take him skiing,
His slope's as slippery
As reasoning freethinkers
Drunk on après-ski,
For he's the champagne anarchist
Who goes off-piste with glee.

And as for education
That dulls you by degree?
He balances equations
With swigs of neat whisky,
For he's a drunkard anarchist
Where one and one make three.

He hates the greedy bankers
Who con us publicly
But freely spends the interest
Accrued mysteriously,
For he's a champagne anarchist
Who's on a spending spree.

Detesting every system,
He hates bureaucracy
But takes the grants and subsidies
That pay for his TV
But any champagne anarchist
Deserves his artist's fee.

He'd close up all the libraries
With verse that's not by him
But counts his words of little worth
And throws them in the bin,
For he's a champagne anarchist
Who takes it on the chin.

He'll help the unknown writer
To notoriety
And shove the Whitbread winner
Beneath the wine dark sea,
Because a champagne anarchist
Despises committee.

He loves to dine in restaurants
That serve *nouvelle cuisine*
Then pay for it on VISA
And call the bill obscene,
For he's a champagne anarchist,
Who never can seem mean.

On trains he travels first class –
Plebs aren't his cup of tea,
And when they ask him what's his drink
Well, guess, it starts with c.
Yes, he's a champagne anarchist
Who always answers *oui*.

And crossing the Atlantic
He's found in business class
Waving to the stewardess
With an empty champagne glass,
For he's a DomPon anarchist
Who never lets fizz pass.

He'll raise himself to heaven
Then close the gates for spite,
He'll write a lyric masterpiece
Then claim his verses trite,
For he's a champagne anarchist
And that's his true birthright.

Yes, I'm that champagne anarchist,
The drinks are all on me
I'll never pay the barman
So don't down one, down three!

Dead

RIDDLED

Riddled? asked his third wife,
Blanching at the news,
Riddled top to toe?
We just got married yesterday,
Fuck me, what a blow.

Riddled, gulped his sister,
Afraid it's in the genes,
Riddled head to toe.
And then she added nervously,
How quickly does it grow?

Riddled? asked young brother,
The doctor nodded "yes".
Riddled top to toe?
"That's not a phrase that I would use
But it's everywhere, ergo..."

Riddled, sung his daughter
Varnishing her nails;
Riddled head to toe.
Then posted it on Instagram
So followers would know.

Riddled, sneered his first wife
Chatting on the phone,
Riddled top to toe.
I'm glad to see the back of him;
I hope he's sent below.

Riddled, pondered Postie,
Pushing junk-mail through street doors,
Riddled head to toe.
We all return to sender,
The celestial PO.

Riddled, nodded neighbours,
Containing their relief,
Riddled top to toe!
And then one questioned eagerly,
You'll sell the bungalow?

Riddled? asked the bookie
Who gave him ten to one.
Riddled head to toe?
He never once touched lucky;
That's how I made my dough.

Riddled, moaned the foreman
With deadlines needing met.
Riddled top to toe.
He was a demon brickie
Despite his vertigo.

Riddled, boomed big Cheryl
Who kissed him once a year,
Riddled head to toe?
I'll miss him come this Christmas
Beneath the mistletoe.

Riddled, whispered Vicar,
The sermon on his mind,
Riddled top to toe.
If that's the way God wills it,
His mysteries to show.

Riddled, mocked the stepson
Locked inside his room.
Riddled head to toe!
I won't be at his burning,
My dad died years ago.

Riddled, mumbled uncle,
Stood beside the hearse,
Riddled top to toe.
Never thought I'd see him here,
Boxed in Walthamstow.

Riddled, said the barmaid
Down the Dog n Duck.
Riddled head to toe.
She poured a shot of whisky.
Have one before you go.

Riddled, smirked the copper
Who felt his collar twice.
Riddled top to toe.
That chancer had it coming
Like every crooked Joe.

Riddled, crooned the DJ
Hosting Tribute Tunes,
Riddled head to toe.
Aunt Bess requests "Addio"
Sung by Alfie Boe.

Riddled, said the banker,
Closing his accounts.
Riddled top to toe,
Then added with subtraction,
At least his debts won't grow.

Riddled, droned Miss Mystic
At her Ouija board,
Riddled head to toe.
I can sense his spirit's
Riddled afterglow!

Riddled, cried the rocker
Who loved him like a dad,
Riddled top to toe.
I'll shout out in his honour
On East End Radio.

Riddled, laughed the comic,
Who knew him as a kid,
Riddled head to toe!
He loved composing riddles:
Who's cold and can't say 'no'?

LAMENT

I'd like to think your days left here
Will fill with one long belly-laugh,
Not the pain and abject fear
That drafts your coming epitaph.

I'd like to think I could be there
To pass your hours with idle chat,
And relatives would measure care
By visiting your tenth floor flat.

You say the telly helps forget
That days like horses race along,
You place a ten bob each-way bet
As hook to hang your mornings on.

When legs permit you make the pub
And watch the dogs through Light 'n' Ben,
But swapping losers is the hub
Of drunken talk for gambling men.

You know that when the cancer eats
To bowel and bone, to spine and brain,
And doctors drop those little cheats:
"You'll soon be up and out again" -

You know that when the thought of food
Or daylight makes you groan and cry,
And nurse becomes a touch less rude -
Your game is up, life's cast the die.

ELEGY

I was nine, he forty-five,
It was Sunday, out for a drive.
I took my ball into this glade.
He stood there suited, bade
Me shoot from ten long yards.
I fired the ball true and hard;
He caught it, threw it back.
I struck again, on the attack.
He palmed it down into the grass
Then caught me with a sneaky pass.
I grabbed the ball; he lifted me
Into this huge oak tree.
The rest's forgot, but why
Do I stand here now and cry?
It happened once, just once, yet tears
Are flowing after fifty years.
And every kick I take today
I run up in that childish way,
Strike with force and vector straight
Then stand and wait
For him to catch my golden shot;
The ball rolls on; Dad does not.

SOLDIER'S SONG

There's a train rolling, rolling
Rolling down the track
It's rolling here for me
Ain't ever coming back

There's a voice calling calling
Calling don't know why
It's calling out for me
To reach up for the sky

There's a dream sleeping sleeping
Sleeping in the night
It's sleeping inside me
Gonna give it light

There's a war raging raging
Raging 'cross the land
It's raging there for me
To fight and make a stand

There's a death waiting waiting
Waiting cold and dark
It's waiting for a young boy
To fall and break your heart

BLUE SKIES BALLAD

The forecast says it's summer,
Blue skies all the way
So I plan to take my mother
Down the shops today.

I draw the bedroom curtain
And peer across the town;
My day becomes less certain
As shells come whining down.

Sirens start a-wailing,
Cars are honking horns
And plumes of smoke are sailing
Above the Town Hall lawns.

I think I'd best get down from here
Before I take a hit
As missiles rocket past my ear
And turn concrete to grit.

I need to reach my mother
On the other side of town
But when I get down lower
I stop and go to ground.

The street is full of soldiers
Rounding up young men,
Soldiers barking orders
Come here! Line up! Fall in!

I crawl behind a bike shed
Then cross the drying green,
Sure that they would shoot me dead
If I should be seen.

Caterpillar tank tracks
Have chewed the tarmac up,
An apartment gaping open cracks
Spews out a bathroom's guts.

Drones declare a travel ban,
The Metro is shutdown,
But I drag a body from a van
To drive across the town.

Its radio's still blaring out
Despite a shrapnel blast,
A wailing woman sings about
Love that cannot last.

Rows of hog-tied corpses
Lie along the road
While massed, invading forces
Seem eager to reload.

I make the open highway
But meet a tank patrol.
It stops me on this blue day
And orders me back home.

I say my mother needs me,
They say she's likely dead.
While pleading with them feebly
They fill me full of lead.

And as I die, I ask them *why*?
One says he's no idea;
The other kneels to close my eyes
And whispers, *cos of fear*.

PLUM BLOSSOM

Quick to shoot, quick to fall,
A shock of sudden blossoms
In unkept grounds, by broken wall
Of long-abandoned homes.

White as brides, the blackened trees
Drop their blooms in showers
To fall on passing refugees
And guns of foreign powers.

LULLABY

I'll walk behind the sinking sun,
Walk to dig a hole,
A hole in heavy clay,
To hollow out a berth
And lay my heartfelt in.
I'll wrap, wrap
Her head in straw
And fold her,
Fold her carefully,
My heartfelt, I shall
Fold and lay
Within the earth,
Within the earth
Where darkness is
Where sun can't rise
Forevermore
Forevermore
Where cock can't crow
Nor lark rise high,
I'll shed a tear
And sing a song
A song so slow, so slow
To plant her in our memories,
To plant her, plant her
Where she cannot grow,
Where songs are spent
In the heartfelt land,
The heartfelt land.

VIXEN

Despite late drunks and passing cops
Or lorries that could squash her flat,
She staggers, dizzy, yawns and stops
Then lollops to the gutter, scats.

Will she feed black crows or worse,
Will binmen dump her in disgust?
By morning light, she never was:
In life there's pain, in death we trust.

WASP

The potter wasp makes an urn
Supplies its yet unborn
With spiders plucked and killed
Before the nest is sealed
And then it flies
Away and dies.

TAMTAN RHYMES

Tamtan of the lonely song
Has one huge eye like a Chinese gong
And seven paws on five short legs,
The forward two like laundry pegs.
It carries its eggs in a leaky sack
Slung across its bowing back.
Its head all bone, its belly scales,
It shuffles leaves with fifteen tails
Feeding on blue rogjam roots
Its gong eye spots in grisham shoots.
It needs to eat a ton each day
Before it builds a bed of clay.
The tamtan only has one use:
Its spittle kills the rungergoose,
So doococks hunt it for its phlegm
Which cakes to form a dooeygem.
Tamtan lives its life alone
And rears one egg into a clone.
Each tam' would live a hundred years
But life drains out in tamtan tears.
Each tear subtracts another day
Of tamtan life expectancy.
So, as by nature deeply sad,
Tam's prognosis tends to bad.
The only thing that cheers it up
Is sunshine from a buttercup
And as it dies it starts to sing -
Some say it is an offering
Though experts state that's clearly wrong
For no-one's ever heard its song.

VALEDICTORY VERSES

How does she, with her dread disease,
Pass the days with jam and cakes?
She's done, has said as much, she shakes
With every *thank you*, *oh* and *please*.

As if the mind won't hear her plea,
The body screams, the brain denies.
She can't pretend, it's in her eyes
But summer's here, let's wait and see.

Days grow further from the truth
As truth comes like a crow to roost;
A knife's an option, so is toast,
Let's choose the latter; death's uncouth.

I loved her once, I held her now gnarled hand,
I kissed her lips, I made her morning tea,
I took her picture everywhere with me.
No-one knows how tomorrow's planned.

Or, in fact, we do but dare not say –
At first its aspirin, then a poultice, then...
You see, the game, it's started once again.
Goodbye, my love, I hope you find your way.

DIRGE

They say her hair was soft as fleece.
I brushed it every day.
Her hair was grey with grief.

They say her eyes shone like the sun.
I watched them noon and night.
Her eyes were dark and dumb.

They say her lips were red like dawn.
I kissed them as she slept.
Her lips were gaunt and drawn.

They say her fingers caressed like silk.
I held them as we wed,
Her fingers cold as milk.

They say her laughter warmed the heart.
I heard it as we danced.
Her laughter tore apart.

They say she loved like Juliet.
I loved her like the sun.
She's never loved me yet.

They say the world wept when she cried.
Her tears were brief as dew.
I said that as she died.

SONGS

I sing with trees at night,
Serenade roots and moonlight.

Or I sing with Sea, whispering
In waves of oceanic lisping.

I learnt to sing in stone
And its cognate, fossilised bone.

I've sung with silver-surging whales;
Beside their song my music pales.

Sky's songs I can't embrace -
Sky duets with empty space.

Human ears and human speech
Strand me on an alien beach.

I fear the song of empty breath
Poets know as death.

Epilogue

HYMN

In garrets, parks, on streets, in pubs,
Down malls, on boats, at transport hubs,
    Let people sing their song.

In quartets, quatrains, quads and choirs,
On canvas, banjo, arranging flowers,
    Let people sing their song.

You can beat me when I'm down
You can run me out of town
Sure I done you wrong
But don't take away my song

In concert halls and galleries,
From mountaintop or in the trees,
    Let people sing their song.

On stages, floats or camper vans,
Through tunnels, hoops or from grandstands,
    Let people sing their song.

Don't take away my song
That's been there all along
Before I saw your eyes
And fell for fortune's lies

As breakdance, jive or ballet corps
On tiptoe crossing ballroom floor,
    Let people sing their song.

In sick bed, prison, by a grave,
At reading, preview or a rave,
    Let people sing their song.

Don't give a damn for me
But singing sets me free
It's more than gold or fame
More cherished than my name

As cantrip, satire, whimper, scream
Flowchart or erotic dream,
    Let people sing their song.

Alone, in crowds, in peace or war,
Alike for workers rich or poor,
    Let people sing their song.

My song is sung for you
Without it we are through
I sing to make us strong
Don't take away our song

Tyrant-crushed or ruled by kings,
Redacted, censored, tied by strings,
    Let people sing their song.

As lion, songbird, whale or angel,
Falsetto from the top of of Babel,
    Let people sing their song.

Best pack my bags and go
You won't enjoy the show
When madness comes along
Because you stole my song

In days to come or time that's been
In heaven, hell or in between,
    Let people sing their song.

Fast forward, play or in reverse
Throughout this glamorous universe,
    Let people sing their song.

Let people sing their song
That's been there all along
Since first our sunlight shone
And words flew off a tongue
Let people sing their song.